AF528450

Beyond the Shadows

Empowering Stories of Resilience and Triumph Over Adversity

Dr Neeta Mhatre

Qurate
quratebooks.com

Book Creation Services

by

BookMyStory®

It's time you tell your story

www.bookmystorypublishing.com

A venture of

R&S Enterprises

Beyond the Shadows

Empowering Stories of Resilience and Triumph Over Adversity

Dr Neeta Mhatre

Published in 2024

© Published by

Qurate qauratebooks.com

Qurate Books Pvt. Ltd.
Goa 403523, India
www.quratebooks.com
Tel: 1800-210-6527, Email: info@quratebooks.com

ISBN: 978-93-58988-53-6

Contents

Preface

There comes a point in life when you're asked to stay strong, even as everything around you falls apart. I've been there–silent when I wanted to scream, resilient when I had no choice but to endure. This book is not just about my journey; it's about finding the strength to rise from the deepest struggles, and to remind you that no matter how impossible the path may seem, you have the power to rebuild.

It's time to break the silence, reach out **Beyond The Shadows,** and find strength in your own voice.

*****

At the tender age of nineteen, my world shifted in ways I could never have imagined. As the youngest child of a protective mother, insecurity had always cast a shadow over our lives. Her decision to marry me off wasn't just about tradition—it was their heartfelt attempt to secure my future, to provide me with the stability she thought I needed. She hoped that marriage would open the door to a life filled with love and promise. But life has its own plans, and what was meant to be a haven soon became a storm I wasn't prepared for. The greener pastures she envisioned seemed to fade, and instead, I found myself navigating a path far from the one I had been promised.

I had no idea what I was stepping into. Marriage—what did it really mean? Was it supposed to bring joy, fulfillment, or something else entirely? All I knew was that I was just nineteen, standing next to a man of twenty-seven, and the weight of the unknown pressed heavily on my shoulders. It was 1995, a time when India was a different world—far from the progressive landscape we see today. Back then, society's expectations were rigid, and the space to question, to express, to even understand one's own needs, was limited. I was too young to grasp the complexities of marriage, too innocent to foresee how drastically my life would change.

Was it the kind of experience one dreams of cherishing forever? For others, perhaps it was—filled with fun, laughter, and endless celebrations. But for me, that joy was fleeting. The happiness that marriage was supposed to bring didn't last beyond five years. In that time, I gave birth to my beautiful daughter, Neha, a moment that remains my most precious gift from those years. But then, the inevitable loomed, and we had to face the harsh reality of filing for divorce. The year was 2000. Just as the world stepped into a new millennium with hope and excitement, I was stepping into a new chapter of my life—one filled with uncertainty, heartbreak, and the daunting task of starting over.

I've walked through the shadowed corridors of family courts, where the air is thick with judgment, and the stares of strangers weigh heavily, silently casting verdicts in their minds. I remember my innocent daughter, just two years old, wide-eyed and confused by the cold, unfamiliar surroundings of the courtroom—while children her age played in parks under the sun. The mental trauma of those moments lingers still, a time when my soul felt shattered and the world seemed cloaked in darkness. My mind was numb, my body out of sync with my thoughts, and all I wanted was to surrender to the overwhelming tide of my circumstances.

Amid this chaos, I received my separation letter. Yet, more than anything, I longed to be heard. But the courtroom isn't a place for stories or emotions. Just as a surgeon cuts open hearts or transplants organs with precision, detached from emotion, the legal process moves with cold efficiency. Family courts sit atop mountains of cases, one stacked upon another, with little room for empathy or understanding. It's not about hearing every cry or every plea—it's about completing one case and swiftly moving on to the next.

I remember one day, during those long nine months of court visits, the lady judge summoned me to her chamber for lunch. It had been six months since the ordeal began, and though her tone was gentle, fear gripped me. In times like these, you brace yourself for more heartbreak, rarely expecting anything good. I was no exception. As I entered, she acknowledged something I hadn't even noticed myself—how I carried myself in the courtroom. With my head down, emotionally torn, I had been dragging myself to court each time, consumed by the weight of it all. She looked at me and said, "I feel sorry for you."

She had seen countless cases like mine, but something about me stood out to her. Most people, she said, seemed shameless or untouched by guilt, but I wasn't like them. I carried my pain visibly, and it struck her deeply. She explained that courts often give people one final opportunity to mend broken bridges, to see if fractured lives can be pieced back together. We were given that chance too.

The court asked me to return to my ex-husband's house, along with my daughter, for a month. It was meant to be a trial—a last effort to see if reconciliation was possible. But just fifteen days in, my daughter and I were thrown out again. Even my innocent, two-year-old child wasn't spared. She was told she would have two mothers—one from Mumbai, and another from somewhere else. In her little world, she thought this was cause for celebration, as if two mothers meant double the joy. But she was too young to understand the reality of what was unfolding.

Eventually, the divorce was finalized. The lady judge had advised me to seek alimony, urging me to think of my daughter's future, but I was resolute. I refused. I didn't want to be tied to the past or rely on anyone to rebuild my life. All I had was six hundred and thirty rupees left in my bank account, and with that, I decided to start over. It wasn't much, but in that moment, I knew there was only one direction left for me—up. I had reached the lowest point, and from there, I had no choice but to rise. My journey into a new life had begun, and with it, a determination to stand on my own, stronger than before.

This book is written with one clear purpose: to inspire those who are ready to go **Beyond The Shadows**. Help is closer than you think. This is not about seeking or even thinking about sympathy—it's about finding the strength to get back up. In these pages, I've brought to light stories of profound depression, mental trauma, the struggles of the LGBTQ community, and society's reluctance to accept these realities. For anyone who resonates with these challenges, I want you to know—you are not alone.

I have made a heartfelt effort to share genuine stories—stories of real people who have faced overwhelming adversity yet found the strength to rise above it. As a psychotherapist, counsellor and trainer, I've had the privilege of walking alongside countless individuals on their journey to healing. This book is dedicated not only to those who have struggled, but especially to those who found the courage to confront their reality and reclaim their lives.

*****

*This book is written with one clear purpose: to inspire those who are ready to go **Beyond The Shadows**. Help is closer than you think. This is not about seeking or even thinking about sympathy—it's about finding the strength to get back up.*

*****

My clients are the true inspiration behind this work. There is no greater reward than witnessing someone open their heart and mind, breaking free from the weight of their past, and transforming into the person they were always destined to be. Their bravery has moved me beyond words, and it is because of their encouragement and trust that I have shared their stories here–stories told with courage, without fear, and with the hope that they inspire others to reach out and do the same.

Over the years, I have been deeply inspired by many books and reading materials that have sparked a profound transformation within me. These works have shaped my understanding, guided my journey, and fuelled my passion to help others. Below are just a few titles that have left an indelible mark on my life:

Rising Strong and Dare to lead: by Brene Brown

The Power of Now by Eckhart Tolle

And small readings of Chinmay Mission helped.

I can only hope that this book, too, will one day be referenced by someone searching for insight, courage, and strength, and that it finds its place on a similar list of books that inspire transformation and growth.

It fills me with immense joy to know that I've been able to make a difference in so many lives–that has become the very purpose of my existence. Helping people realize that no matter how dark the moment, it's not the end of the world, has been my greatest reward. In a world where mental health issues are still burdened by stigma, many people hesitate to come forward, trapped by the fear of judgment or misunderstanding. I want people to know that seeking help is a sign of strength, not weakness, and she encourages anyone struggling to reach out, embrace support, and begin their journey toward healing.

This book, long in the making, had to be published now, in celebration of a significant milestone—my fiftieth birthday this November.

Today, having found happiness again through remarriage, I've finally come into my own, both personally and professionally. My purpose is clear, and my heart is full.

So, come—go **Beyond The Shadows**. Break the chains that hold you back, for the world is waiting for you to unleash the real, unshackled version of yourself.

The journey to evolve begins here. The time is now.

Key Takeaways:

- **Courage to Rise:** Life's most difficult moments aren't the end—they are often the start of something new. This book encourages you to find the strength within yourself to rise above adversity.

- **Reach Out:** Help is always within reach. Whether you're dealing with depression, trauma, or societal challenges, you don't have to face it alone—there's always someone ready to listen.

- **Empowerment Over Sympathy:** The goal is not to seek sympathy but to empower yourself to evolve. This book shares stories of people who found their way forward by confronting their reality, not shrinking from it.

Where else did you connect? If any of these stories or ideas resonate with you, know that you're not alone.

This is your moment to break free, reach out, go **Beyond The Shadows** and step into your true self.

> Here are a few celebrities who have overcome immense challenges and stressful situations to rise to the top of their fields. Despite facing personal and professional setbacks, their stories are a testament to resilience and the power of perseverance. These individuals didn't let adversity define them, and today, they stand as icons of success, inspiring countless others with their journeys.

J.K. Rowling (Author)

- Before she became a global literary sensation with "*Harry Potter,*" J.K. Rowling went through a challenging divorce from her first husband, Jorge Arantes. At one point, she was a single mother on welfare. Her story is one of true perseverance, showing how she rebuilt her life from hardship to unimaginable success.

Kiran Mazumdar-Shaw (Founder of Biocon)

- Kiran Mazumdar-Shaw, a successful entrepreneur and chairperson of Biocon, went through a divorce. She has been a trailblazer in the biotechnology industry, advocating for affordable healthcare and women's empowerment in business.

Foreword

I came to know Dr. Neeta through her mother, Dr. Mrs. Gomati Mishra, who was a patient of mine, suffering from ischemic heart disease. Living close to my clinic, she was under my care for many years. As a family physician with over 35 years of experience—initially trained in the ICCU at Sir H.N. Hospital, Girgaum, before transitioning to general practice—I have had the privilege of watching Dr. Neeta's journey unfold.

In her early days, Neeta kept herself busy doing medicals for seafarers and volunteering at various NGOs. She arranged medical camps for the underprivileged, always finding ways to help others in need. Her journey has been marked by personal highs and lows, especially through her mother's illness and eventual passing. It took time for her to come to terms with this loss, but today, she is thriving. She has found her calling and has grown tremendously, both professionally and personally.

In her work, Dr. Neeta is dedicated to helping people on their mental health journeys, offering her services both one-on-one and through group sessions. Her empathy and genuine ability to listen have created strong bonds with her clients. Neeta is not only committed to her profession, she has also grown spiritually, becoming more God-loving than God-fearing. She strives to cause no harm and remains open-hearted, often giving people second chances without holding onto grudges.

Her commitment to listening stems, in part, from her own experience with a court-appointed counsellor who didn't offer the support or time she needed. This drove her to be the kind of counsellor she once needed—a compassionate, patient, and attentive guide for those in need.

Among the stories in this book, my favourite is the chapter on Sona. Sona was a patient of mine, and on a particularly dark day, she suffered a severe attack at home. Neeta was the only one who could reach through the chaos to Sona, convincing her to get the help she needed. Watching Sona's remarkable progress since then has been incredibly rewarding and is a testament to Neeta's ability to make a lasting impact.

Dr. Neeta's journey is one of resilience, compassion, and growth. Her dedication to supporting others through their darkest times is inspiring, and I am certain that this book will offer hope and insight to many. My best wishes to her as she continues to make a difference, one life at a time.

Dr. Srikant Mhatre

Family Physician

Introduction

I was born in the bustling city of Mumbai, but life took a heart-breaking turn almost before it had even begun. Just six months after I came into this world, I lost my father. At that tender age, I was too young to grasp the gravity of the loss, but it quietly shaped the course of my life, casting a shadow that followed me for years. We were a family of four siblings, yet today, that number has diminished—my brother passed away some years ago, leaving just my two sisters and me. Growing up, I carried an unspoken burden of guilt. I was the youngest, the most pampered, and perhaps because I never had the chance to know my father, my mother lavished extra care on me. She became both my mother and my father, her love fierce and protective, but behind her strength, I always felt the weight of her worry—for my future, for our family, for everything that had been lost.

As a child, I would watch other kids being dropped off at school by their fathers, and a quiet confusion would well up inside me. I'd wonder, *Why isn't my life like theirs*? I would search for answers that no one seemed to have. It was always our maid, Shantibai who took me to school, and though she was kind, the absence of my father was something I felt deeply, even if I couldn't fully understand it at the time. The sight of fathers hugging their children goodbye or waving proudly from the school gates left me with an ache I couldn't quite name. Why was my life so different? That emptiness lingered in my mind, a quiet shadow that followed me everywhere.

Despite this emotional turmoil, I poured myself into my studies, as if by excelling academically, I could somehow fill the void. For a long time, my books became my refuge—a place where the confusion and pain of my reality didn't touch me. School was where I could escape, even if only for a little while.

During my school years, I began to notice something that set me apart—my peers listened to me. As a member of the Scout & Guide I was often the one they turned to for help, knowing I would always lend a compassionate ear. I was approachable, someone they could trust, and this gave me a quiet sense of purpose. Little did I know then that this trait—being a good listener—would become one of my greatest strengths and would profoundly shape my career in the years to come. What began as a simple willingness to help others evolved into a foundational skill that would guide me through my professional journey.

But life, as it often does, threw me another turning point in the 10th grade—one that would change everything.

When we moved to a new school, I quickly found myself feeling out of place. The environment was unfamiliar, and the warmth I had known before seemed to vanish. It wasn't long before a deep sense of inferiority began to take root within me. I was constantly reminded, in subtle and not-so-subtle ways, that I didn't belong—that I wasn't part of this tribe. It was as though the world around me had decided that I wasn't good enough, and slowly, I began to believe it too.

Amidst all the chaos and mental trauma I was experiencing, there was always one constant—my mother. She was my pillar of strength, a beacon of resilience in my darkest moments. As a general practitioner, my mother wasn't just a doctor; she was a healer in every sense of the word. I watched her care for not only me and my siblings but also our home, all while carrying the weight of losing her husband at such a young age. Despite her own struggles, she remained unwavering in her dedication to her work, treating patients with sincerity and compassion. Many times, if someone couldn't afford to pay, she'd treat them free of charge, without hesitation. Her honesty, integrity, and selflessness were values that imprinted on me, shaping who I am today, and they continue to guide me in everything I do.

After completing school, I decided to pursue Science in my graduation, with dreams of following in my mother's footsteps. I enrolled for the Pre-Medical exams, but when I fell short of the required seven hundred marks, my path took a different turn.

I chose to explore alternative systems of medicine, eventually gravitating toward homeopathy. During this period, my mother's health began to decline. She was battling cardiac issues, but what seemed to weigh on her more than her physical ailments was her worry for my future. The doctor who treated her believed that her concern for me—knowing that my siblings might not be there to support me—was at the heart of her condition. It was a realization that shook me deeply, as I saw the profound impact her love and worry had on her health.

In the midst of all this, my mother's greatest concern became my marriage. Knowing her health was failing, she called my father's family to meet her, along with my siblings—who were almost twelve years older than me. With no brother or father in the family, the absence of a male figure loomed large, especially when it came to traditional expectations like marriage. My mother expressed her fears, and it was collectively decided that they would begin searching for a suitable match. However, the reality of not having a male figure to provide dowry or cover the wedding expenses was a challenge we all understood. The solution seemed to be arranging my marriage back in our native place, where proposals would be more accessible.

And so, at the tender age of nineteen, I was married in Benares, Uttar Pradesh. It was a far cry from the world I knew, where my brother was a doctor and my uncles were esteemed cardiologists and gynaecologists. In my native town, such educational backgrounds were rare, but the weight of expectations and tradition guided the decision. My life, in many ways, was shaped by these circumstances beyond my control.

Within one year of our marriage, we moved back to Mumbai, as my ex-husband sought better prospects for settling down. It was during this time that Neha was born. While her arrival brought immense joy into my life, I couldn't help but notice his growing detachment. He rarely participated in her activities, and our conversations were often strained, filled with unspoken frustrations and widening gaps in communication. Despite the hope that a fresh start in Mumbai might bring us closer, it became clear that something fundamental was missing.

Not long after, he returned to Allahabad to pursue the Indian Engineering Services and was eventually posted to Lucknow. I moved with Neha to join him, but the distance between us—both emotional and physical—continued to grow. What had once been small cracks in our relationship had now become unbridgeable divides. After much reflection, we both acknowledged that our paths were no longer aligned, and with heavy hearts, we made the decision to part ways and proceed with the divorce.

Neha endured more than I could have imagined on this journey. In the early years, she was blissfully unaware of the complexities of our situation, but as she grew older, the impact of my decisions began to shape her life. I vividly remember the day she came home unexpectedly from school, her behaviour startling my mother. Sensing something was wrong, I rushed back from work, where I was fortunate to have a supportive boss who always encouraged me to stay strong and saw potential in me. He believed that one day I would emerge stronger and successful, but nothing could have prepared me for what Neha said that day.

With tears in her eyes, she looked at me and said, "You are a liar." Her words cut through me like a blade. Neha had always assumed that no one at school knew about the absence of her father. But that day, she was asked in front of her classmates to speak about her experience living with only a mother, with no father figure in her life. It was a devastating moment for her, one that left a scar not just on her heart, but on our relationship.

For years after that, the connection between us frayed. I became nothing more than a “provider” in her eyes—someone who met her needs but didn’t share the bond that mothers and daughters usually do. The emotional distance between us widened, and it wasn’t until she turned fourteen that she began to understand the complexity of our situation. Until then, the closeness we had once shared was lost, buried beneath the weight of unspoken pain and unresolved emotions.

There came a time when Neha, now more mature and perceptive, expressed a desire for us to have a complete family. She felt that I needed to remarry. My mother, too, shared the same sentiment, believing that I deserved a second chance at happiness. While society may have grown to accept remarriages in principle, the reality was far more complicated, and I found myself facing unexpected obstacles and judgments.

Having a daughter, Neha, was seen by many not as the beautiful blessing she was, but as a liability. In the eyes of some, she wasn’t a cherished part of my life, but an "additional burden"—something no one would willingly take on. These harsh perceptions left me shaken, as the worth of my daughter, my love, and my experiences were diminished by shallow societal expectations. It was as though being a single mother disqualified me from the possibility of a fresh start, and the idea that a woman with a child could seek happiness seemed too far-fetched for some to accept.

*****

While society may have grown to accept remarriages in principle, the reality was far more complicated, and I found myself facing unexpected obstacles and judgments.

*****

But life, as it often does, had different plans for me. My mother's doctor, Srikant, who had been treating her for her cardiac issues, slowly became a part of my life in ways I hadn't expected. He too had gone through the pain of loss and from 2006 to 2009 due to my mother's treatment with him, we remained in constant touch and often met at his clinic. One day, my mother, in her characteristic directness, asked him if he would consider marrying me. To my surprise, he agreed, and in 2011, we became engaged.

We gave ourselves plenty of time to truly get to know one another, ensuring that our families, too, felt comfortable with the union. What mattered most to me, however, was how Srikant and his family embraced Neha with open arms. Watching his family and him bond with her, seeing her finally accepted without question or hesitation, brought a level of peace I hadn't felt in years. It was as though the missing pieces of our family were finally falling into place.

Srikant blended seamlessly into my family, and soon, what had once felt broken now felt complete. Neha's joy was infectious—she was beaming with happiness, and I could see her excitement as she began planning every detail of the wedding. From the *haldi* to the *mehendi*, from the baraat to the ceremony itself, she made sure our wedding had all the elements of a grand celebration. It was as if, after all the challenges we had faced, we were finally stepping into the life we were meant to live.

But just two years after my marriage, my mother passed away. As unbelievable as it sounds, she had once told me that she would only live for two years after seeing me settled. It was as if she had known all along, as though her life's final chapter was tied to ensuring that I had found happiness and stability. Her passing left a void that could never be filled, but her love and strength continued to guide me. She had fulfilled her promise to stay until I was truly settled, and though her physical presence was gone, I carried her spirit with me—her unwavering love, her resilience, and her belief in me that now became my guiding light.

*****

But just two years after my marriage, my mother passed away. As unbelievable as it sounds, she had once told me that she would only live for two years after seeing me settled.

*****

After earning my Master's in Social Welfare, my journey as a counsellor began to take shape, and for a while, life seemed to be falling into place. As a family, we found ourselves in a good space—financially stable and emotionally secure. It felt like the years of hardship were finally behind us. But life, in its unpredictable way, had other plans.

In 2019, life took an unexpected turn when Srikant's health began to decline. It was during the COVID-19 times, between 2019 and 2021, he faced serious health challenges, but through it all, we fought as a family. It was a difficult time, but his strength and our collective resilience helped us navigate through those dark days.

It was as if everything was collapsing all at once. The world outside was crumbling under the weight of the pandemic, while inside, our home was filled with the deafening silence of uncertainty. Srikant, once full of life and strength, now lay weak and frail. Each hospital visit felt like stepping into the unknown, and I had to summon every ounce of resilience I had left just to make it through the day. I was no stranger to adversity, but this was different—this was personal, and it was relentless.

The toll it took on Neha and me was immeasurable. There were sleepless nights, moments of quiet tears, and the overwhelming burden of trying to stay strong for each other. Yet, amidst the darkness, we found glimmers of hope. Slowly, with each passing day, Srikant began to heal. The journey was far from over, but there was light at the end of the tunnel—a faint, yet undeniable, light.

Today, Srikant continues to practice his profession, physically weaker but mentally unbroken. Neha has found her footing in her career, and I've returned to my role as a Psychotherapist &Counsellor, with a renewed sense of purpose.

But the scars remain. This experience tested our strength and resilience in ways I never thought possible, yet it also gave me a deeper understanding of the fragility of life, and the importance of holding on—no matter how rough the storm.

In many ways, my journey has come full circle. Everything I've gone through—the struggles, the heartbreak, the moments of doubt—has shaped me into the person I am today. Each trial has been a stepping stone, moulding my resilience and teaching me lessons I never anticipated. From the loss of my father at an early age, the painful years of a marriage that couldn't survive, to the battles fought alongside Shrikant, I've come to understand that suffering doesn't define you, but how you rise from it does. These experiences have given me a clarity of purpose that I hold close to my heart: no other woman, no other "Neeta," should have to suffer in silence.

I know the crushing weight of feeling alone, of carrying burdens that seem too heavy to bear. I've lived it. And I've learned that even in the darkest moments, the smallest acts of kindness, the simplest gesture of understanding, can be a lifeline. That's why I'm determined to be there for those who feel abandoned by the world, for those who think they have no one to turn to. I want to be the voice that reminds them they're not alone, the hand that reaches out when they feel they're sinking.

Through my journey as a counsellor, I've seen the transformative power of listening—really listening. It's not about fixing someone's life in an instant, but about offering a safe space, a shoulder to lean on, and the knowledge that someone truly cares. I've learned that empathy can heal in ways no medication ever could. Sometimes, people don't need solutions right away; they need someone who is willing to stand beside them as they navigate their pain.

My mission has become clear: I want to be a light for others, to help them find their strength when they feel they have none left. I want to give hope to those who feel trapped in despair, to show them that even though the road may be long, they don't have to walk it alone. My experiences have taught me that we can't always choose the battles life throws at us, but we can choose how we face them. And I want to help others face theirs with courage, knowing that support is always within reach.

For every woman who feels lost, for every individual who's on the verge of giving up, I want to offer a hand and say, "I see you, and I'm here for you." It's a mission that extends far beyond my own story, because I believe that together, we can break the silence that often surrounds suffering. We can create a world where no one has to endure pain in isolation.

It's a mission rooted in love, empathy, and the belief that sometimes, all it takes is one person to show up and remind you of your worth. And if I can be that person for someone, then everything I've endured has been worth it.

In the following pages, I bring to you real stories from my clients—individuals who have bravely allowed me to share their emotions, their struggles, and their triumphs. Each story is a testament to the resilience of the human spirit, showcasing the unique challenges they faced and the profound pain they endured. I've been there; I've seen it all. Their journeys resonate deeply with my own, reminding me of the power of vulnerability and the strength that emerges from sharing one's truth.

These stories are not just tales of hardship; they are chronicles of transformation. They illustrate how each person confronted their trauma head-on, fought through the darkness, and emerged stronger on the other side. From battling anxiety and depression to navigating the complexities of relationships and personal loss, these individuals have faced their fears and have chosen to reclaim their lives.

You will read about their journeys of self-discovery, their moments of despair, and the light that flickered within them, guiding them toward healing. With every page, you'll witness their resilience, their determination to change their circumstances, and the pivotal moments that sparked their transformation. These are stories filled with hope, reminding us that even in the bleakest times, change is possible.

As you delve into their experiences, I invite you to reflect on your own journey. What challenges have you faced? What stories resonate with you? Through these narratives, I hope you find inspiration, strength, and the understanding that you are not alone. My mission is to save lives, one story at a time, by being there—truly being there—for those who need it most.

I also extend my sincere gratitude to all my mentors, teachers, parents, well-wishers, and the various circumstances that have contributed to my growth.

So, as you turn the pages ahead, prepare to be moved. Allow yourself to connect with the emotions laid bare, the struggles shared, and the victories celebrated. Each story is a reminder that while the road to healing may be long and winding, it is also filled with moments of courage and triumph. Together, we can learn from these journeys, embrace our own stories, and find solace in the knowledge that hope is always within reach.

Write to me at: **drneeta.neha@gmail.com**

Words of Gratitude

"Dr Neeta has curated real life stories that move us beyond measure. She compassionately exhibits how there is always hope, even in lives that are often lived on the fringes of society, marred by deep rooted biases and traumatised by stereotypes. I am glad these stories now reach many. My wish is they nudge soul searching within us as a society and inspire us to become more inclusive in every way."

Shilpa Ajwani

Founder & CEO unomantra

Former MD Tupperware India

*****

“Warm, friendly and approachable - Dr Neeta is the right choice for anyone who is looking for a Mental Health expert. Her patient hearing enables the client to open up and pour their heart out as they feel enveloped in a compassionate embrace of comforting words and wise advice.

Dr. Neeta's vast experience and exposure in various forms of therapies allows her to intuitively use the therapy that is best applicable for the client.

She is one person I can blindly recommend anyone who needs therapy.

My best wishes to her in all her endeavours.”

Arpita Ghosh

Centre Head for Counselling and Health Services

CHRIST (Deemed to be) University Lavasa Pune

*****

“Dr Neeta Mhatre is a person with remarkable perception and empathy. Her kindness toward challenged people, whether it be the LGBTQ community, or people facing mental health challenges, is exemplary. I am positive that her book will inspire many and will bring joy and relief to many. I wish her the very best for her book.”

Milind Kher

ICF Certified Life Coach and Emotional Intelligence Specialist.

*****

"I have had the privilege of collaborating with Dr. Neeta Mishra-Mhatre on several training projects, and her impact has been nothing short of transformational. Dr. Neeta brings a unique blend of psychic insight, healing expertise, and deep empathy to her work, which creates a truly holistic and impactful experience for those she engages with. Personally, I have greatly benefited from her guidance; her advice is always timely, wise, and transformative.

Dr. Neeta's dedication extends beyond professional boundaries, as she has made remarkable contributions to social work, particularly in supporting destitute girls across India. Her commitment to uplifting others is evident in every aspect of her work. Feedback from participants about her training style has consistently been positive, highlighting her ability to inspire meaningful growth and change. I am grateful for the opportunity to know and work alongside such a remarkable healer and visionary."

Regards,

Sarang Yande

Senior Advisor, Capability Workforce Strategy, Ministry of Business, Innovation and Employment, Government of New Zealand

*****

I am deeply grateful for the profound impact of Dr. Neeta has had on my personal and professional growth.

As a psychotherapist and trainer, her expertise and compassionate approach have been invaluable, particularly in her work with the LGBTQ community.

Dr. Neeta creates a safe and inclusive environment where individuals can explore their identities and challenges without fear of judgment.

Her ability to listen and understand is unparalleled; she provides insights that not only foster self-acceptance but also empower individuals to embrace their authentic selves.

Through her mentoring, I have gained practical tools and strategies that have enhanced my understanding of diversity and inclusion and growth in personal and professional space.

She is a passionate advocate for mental health and well-being, and her commitment to the LGBTQ community shines through in everything she does.

I wholeheartedly recommend Dr. Neeta for her upcoming book.

Her wisdom and experience will undoubtedly resonate with many, and her dedication to fostering understanding and acceptance is truly inspiring. She is an inspiration to many.

Heartiest Congratulations Dr. Neeta and keep Blooming and Inspiring.

Best wishes for your future endeavours.

God bless you

Much love

Payal Irani ♥
Bloom
Founder and CEO

My Turn to Shield: A Daughter's Promise

In the corridor of my memories, I journey through the hazy recollections of my childhood, exploring the profound impact my mother has had on my life. Each step down the corridors of my past brings me closer to the struggles and sorrows she endured–each memory standing as a testament to her resilience and unwavering strength.

From her humble beginnings, my mother became my hero, a figure of grace and perseverance who navigated life's storms with quiet dignity. Her strength was a beacon in times of turbulence, teaching me the invaluable lessons of courage, love, and resilience. Those moments of hardship shaped not only her but also me, granting me a deep understanding of her sacrifices and instilling a strength of my own.

Today, I look at her with immense respect, love, and pride. She is the unshakeable pillar of my life, the backbone of my existence. This book celebrates her journey—a lotus blooming from the muddy waters of the past, rising above every challenge to stand tall and beautiful. It is a tribute to her indomitable spirit and to the incredible influence she has had in shaping the person I am today. Through her, I learned that true strength lies in facing adversity head-on, and for that, I am eternally grateful.

Dr. Neeta Mhatre is more than just my mother; she is my mentor, my guide, and my best friend. She has taught me to seek solutions rather than dwell on problems—a lesson that has become my guiding mantra. Whenever I face challenges, I find myself asking, "What would she do?" Her resilience and unwavering spirit continue to inspire me to confront difficulties with courage.

Now, it is my turn to support her, to share in the responsibilities and walk alongside her as she continues her journey. I want nothing more than to see her flourish, to bloom like a flower basking in sunlight, free from the burdens she once carried. Together, we face the future hand in hand, bound by love, respect, and gratitude. This narrative is not only a celebration of her journey but also a testament to the transformative power of maternal love.

As I hold my mother close, I feel a deep sense of responsibility and love. It's my turn now to be her shield, to cover her as she has always covered me. For years, she stood as my protector, my guide through every storm. Today, I embrace the role of standing by her side, providing the same strength and support she has given me. I ask for God's strength to uphold her, to be the anchor she has been for me, and to ensure she feels safe, cherished, and loved. Together, we face life hand-in-hand, each of us a guardian for the other.

Dr. Neha Mishra, a.k.a. "*Banchu*" for my mother

The Mirror of Self-Love:

Ritu's Path to Empowerment

When Ritu first walked into Dr. Neeta, the mindset was different. It wasn't about seeking sympathy or grappling with confusion—Ritu had already accepted and embraced his identity as a non-binary trans person. But despite that self-awareness, Ritu was still carrying the heavy burden of finding oneself, societal judgment and internalized expectations. The weight of years spent navigating a world that often didn't understand or accept Ritu had left a mark. Ritu wasn't lost, but needed help letting go of the pain and finding the strength to being loved fully, beyond the limits that others had placed on him.

As a non-binary trans person navigating a world that often felt cold and unwelcoming, Ritu's confidence had been worn down by years of harsh societal judgment and internal battles. The strength he once had to stand tall in their truth had slowly eroded under the weight of expectations, prejudice, and the quiet ache of being misunderstood. When Ritu came to Dr. Neeta, he wasn't just seeking answers– Ritu was searching for a lifeline, for someone who could help him reclaim the parts of himself that had been buried beneath doubt and fear. It was clear that Ritu's sense of self-love had been lost along the way, and more than anything, Ritu needed someone as a guide, to help reignite the light that once shone so brightly within.

A non-binary trans person doesn't fit neatly into society's conventional understanding of male or female. They may identify as both, neither, or some fluid combination of the two. For some, their identity shifts—feeling more masculine on some days, more feminine on others, or existing somewhere entirely outside the binary spectrum. It's a deeply personal and evolving experience that can be difficult for others to grasp, often leading to confusion and misunderstanding.

Ritu had come to a place of understanding his body and the emotions it had gone through. Ritu had embraced the fluidity of his identity, knowing that it wasn't about fitting into predefined categories but about living authentically in his own skin. While the world around Ritu struggled to understand, Ritu had already made peace with his identity. The challenge, however, was shedding the emotional weight of societal expectations and learning how to love and prioritize themselves in a world that didn't always accept them for who they were.

I first met Ritu at an event organized by an NGO where I was working closely with the transgender community. Ritu had heard about me through various sources and was eager to connect, hoping to embark on a journey of self-discovery. From the moment we spoke, I could sense a deep desire for growth within Ritu. He wasn't seeking sympathy or validation, Ritu was ready to help himself and fully committed to the process of therapy. But there were two conditions: absolute confidentiality, and no judgment, not even from me. Only then, Ritu said, would he feel safe enough to truly express himself.

From the very beginning, there was something about Ritu that stood out. It wasn't just the way Ritu articulated the thoughts or the courage it took to approach me with such clarity about his conditions–it was the unmistakable spark in Ritu's eyes. There was a quiet intensity, a determination that radiated beneath the surface, even in those first few conversations. It was as if Ritu had already fought through the confusion that so often clouds self-discovery and was now standing at the edge, ready to leap, but just needed the right direction.

In every session, that spark became more evident. Ritu wasn't merely attending therapy– but was fully engaged, bringing an energy and eagerness to each meeting that was contagious. Ritu would arrive early, prepared, with a notebook in hand, ready to absorb every word and apply it to his life. Ritu's questions were thoughtful, and reflections were deep. This wasn't someone passively waiting for change to happen–Ritu was actively seeking it, hungry for growth. Every task I gave Ritu, were tackled with enthusiasm and purpose. Ritu didn't just follow my guidance; but made it his own, constantly looking for ways to better, pushing boundaries, and exploring his potential.

It was clear that Ritu had a fire within him, a drive to not only accept who he was but to thrive in that identity. Ritu wasn't afraid of hard work, nor was he deterred by the challenges ahead. Where others might have faltered, Ritu leaned in, showing a resilience and determination that was truly inspiring. There was no doubt in my mind that with this kind of passion, Ritu was destined to achieve great things.

Even when the journey became difficult–and there were certainly moments when it did–Ritu's spark never dimmed. Instead, it grew brighter, as if every challenge only fuelled his resolve to rise above it. Ritu didn't just want to discover himself–he wanted to create a version of himself that was powerful, confident, and capable of standing tall in a world that often tried to diminish him. And Ritu did exactly that.

But beneath Ritu's spark and determination lay a constant struggle–a fight not just within but with the world around. Ritu was navigating a society that often failed to understand or accept his identity as a non-binary trans person. Every day felt like a battle to carve out a space where he could truly belong. The questions weighed heavily on Ritu: *How do I tell people that I am non-binary? Will they even understand? How will I be seen—will I be accepted, or constantly judged?*

These weren't just passing doubts; they were deep-seated fears, rooted in years of societal judgment. Ritu had already fought the internal war of self-acceptance, but now Ritu had to face the external world—a world that often clung to rigid definitions of gender, leaving little room for someone like him. There was an ever-present anxiety: *Would people respect my identity, or would they dismiss me as an outsider? How will I be taken in professional settings?*

The corporate world, in particular, loomed large in Ritu's mind. How could Ritu find his place in a business landscape that still held traditional views of gender? How would he navigate office spaces, boardrooms, and networking events where the lines between male and female were so starkly drawn? And even more daunting, what would happen when he decided to take a bigger leap—to step out on his own as an entrepreneur? The path ahead seemed fraught with obstacles, and every potential opportunity felt like it was shadowed by the uncertainty of how he would be perceived.

*****

But beneath Ritu's spark and determination lay a constant struggle—a fight not just with himself but with the world around him. Ritu was navigating a society that often failed to understand or accept his identity as a non-binary trans person.

*****

Ritu wasn't just worried about success; he was worried about how his identity would influence that success. The thought of introducing himself in meetings, of explaining *who he was—a non-binary trans person*–filled him with dread. There was always that lingering question: *Will they understand? Or will I be dismissed before I even get a chance to prove myself?*

These doubts gnawed at him, creating an ongoing internal dilemma. Ritu knew he had the passion, the skills, and the drive to succeed–but how could Ritu rise above the societal judgments that seemed to block his path? How could he find the courage to fully embrace his identity, not just in his personal life, but in the professional world, and ultimately, as a leader and entrepreneur?

While Ritu had come to terms with his identity, the journey was far more complex when it came to Ritu's family. Ritu's father, though initially confused, had come to accept Ritu for who he was, quietly supporting his child in whatever way he could. But the situation with his mother was different–painfully different. She couldn't reconcile Ritu's identity with the expectations she had held for years. In her heart, she desperately clung to the hope that Ritu would become like everyone else, like the son she had imagined–someone who fit neatly into society's norms, someone she could proudly present to the world.

Her love for Ritu was undeniable, but it was a love that struggled to understand, a love clouded by fear, confusion, and societal pressure. She turned to what she knew best–faith and tradition. Filled with emotion and a growing sense of helplessness, she relied on religious ceremonies, believing they could somehow "cure"

Ritu, make him "whole" in the way she had envisioned. It was her way of trying to fix what she didn't yet understand, convinced that through ritual and prayer, her child could be saved from the life she feared would be filled with rejection and hardship.

*****

Ritu's father, though initially confused, had come to accept Ritu for who he was, quietly supporting his child in whatever way he could. But the situation with his mother was different—painfully different. She couldn't reconcile Ritu's identity with the expectations she had held for years.

*****

For Ritu, this was a harrowing experience. Every ceremony, every prayer, felt like another attempt to erase the person he was–another denial of his true self. Ritu wasn't broken, but the mother's desperation made Ritu feel as if he was. She sought the help of spiritual healers, dragging Ritu through countless rituals that left him emotionally drained. Each time, Ritu hoped for her to see him, to accept him as he was, not as someone who needed to be "fixed." Yet the more she clung to these practices, the more isolated Ritu felt, caught between his identity and his mother's unwavering desire for him to conform.

It wasn't just the ceremonies that weighed on him–it was the emotional toll of seeing his mother suffer, watching her tears as she prayed for a transformation that would never come. Ritu loved her deeply, and the conflict between wanting to stay true to himself and not wanting to hurt his mother was agonizing. Ritu knew that her intentions came from a place of love and fear—fear that the world wouldn't accept him, that he would face a life filled with pain and rejection. But what she didn't realize was that the very process of trying to change Ritu was causing more harm than any outside judgment ever could.

In those moments, Ritu wasn't just struggling for his own acceptance—Ritu was struggling to reconcile his love for his mother with her inability to accept him as he was. It was a heart-breaking experience, knowing that the person who gave him life couldn't yet see the life he was trying to live. The journey was painful, for both of them, as they navigated the complexities of love, identity, and the unrelenting pressure of societal expectations.

For Ritu, I knew that a tailored approach was necessary—one that combined various therapeutic tools to help Ritu navigate his unique journey. I drew from my expertise in **Gestalt Therapy, NLP, and Basic Counselling Techniques**, all of which played crucial roles in addressing the emotional layers Ritu had built over time. But beyond the structured techniques, I found that **Art Based Therapy and Metaphor Therapy** also became an essential outlet for Ritu's self-expression.

Each of these methods served as stepping stones, helping him not only to explore his inner world but to begin embracing the parts of himself that had been hidden for so long. It was through this holistic approach—merging mind, body, and creativity—that Ritu's journey toward self-acceptance and empowerment truly took shape.

*****

- **Gestalt Therapy** - A psychotherapy that helps people understand themselves and their relationship by focusing on the present moment.
- **NLP-** Neuro Linguistic Programming: is an approach to communication, personal development, phobias, fears, managing emotions by changing the language pattern.
- **Counselling -** It's a professional help and advice given to the client to resolve personal, professional, psychological and social problems.
- **ABT-** Arts Based Therapy: is a creative therapeutic practice which helps people express themselves and improve their mental health. Good tool for mood enhancement.
- **Metaphor Therapy:** involves delving into drawing analysis, utilizing these unique projective techniques to explore and interpret a client's emotions and subconscious thoughts through symbolic imagery.

*****

I applied all of these techniques with Ritu, and over time, the transformation was remarkable. Slowly but surely, Ritu began to shed the weight of past traumas and fears, and what emerged was a confident, empowered individual. The horrors that once haunted him no longer held him back. Ritu's mind became focused, clear, and directed toward his passion—Ritu's dream of building a clothing manufacturing venture. With each session, I could see Ritu stepping into his true potential, gaining not just self-love but the ambition and drive to succeed.

Today, under his brand *Reeti*, Ritu is a thriving entrepreneur in the glamorous world of fashion. A collection of fusion dresses beautifully reflects Ritu's journey—bold, creative, and unapologetically unique. The very world that once felt distant and unwelcoming is now one where Ritu shines, a testament to his resilience and determination. Ritu has turned his vision into reality, creating a brand that not only represents his identity but also inspires others to embrace their own.

Unlike many cases I've handled, where the counselling begins with helping individuals come to terms with their bodies, Ritu's journey was different. He had already embraced his identity as a non-binary trans person. Ritu didn't come to me seeking acceptance; he came looking for direction—on how to structure his life, find purpose, and set clear goals. This clarity of purpose made my therapy with him focused and intentional, as we worked on building the framework for a life he envisioned.

Today, Ritu often reaches out to update me on his progress, sharing what's happening in his life and what lies ahead. Ritu's outlook is vibrant and positive, and his ambition has only grown. Ritu confidently tells me that soon, his name will be all over the news, and I don't doubt it for a moment. Ritu's success is a true feather in my cap, something I hold close with immense pride.

*****

Unlike many cases I've handled, where the counselling begins with helping individuals come to terms with their bodies, Ritu's journey was different. Ritu had already embraced his identity as a non-binary trans person. Ritu didn't come to me seeking acceptance; he came looking for direction—on how to structure his life, find purpose, and set clear goals.

*****

More than anything, I hope that Ritu's story inspires other non-binary trans people to step out of the shadows, to embrace their identities, and to pursue their dreams without fear. Ritu's journey is a powerful reminder that with the right support, we can all become the best versions of ourselves.

****

I want to take a moment to reflect on my association with TISS–Tata Institute of Social Sciences. This prestigious multi-campus public university in Mumbai is Asia's oldest institution for professional social work education, founded in 1936.

As a guest faculty there, I had the privilege of conducting a program on **Transpreneurship**. It was a transformative gathering, bringing together over a few hundred transgender individuals, for whom TISS arranged accommodations and support to help them participate in the program. The experience was deeply satisfying, as I witnessed first-hand the eagerness of these individuals to learn and empower themselves. Their willingness to engage in this journey was a testament to their fighting spirit and determination to live fulfilling, authentic lives.

When I compare my experience counselling Ritu with my time at TISS, I find a powerful synergy. The theoretical knowledge I gained at TISS informed my practice, allowing me to help Ritu apply those concepts in real life, leading to meaningful results. Ritu's journey exemplifies the essence of empowerment that we discussed at TISS. Ritu emerged from the shadows of uncertainty and self-doubt, ready to embrace his identity and pursue dreams with unwavering confidence.

Ultimately, both experiences have reinforced my belief in the transformative power of education and support. Ritu's success and the resilience of those at TISS inspire me to continue this vital work, fostering a world where every individual can step into the light and live authentically. Together, we are creating pathways to empowerment, and I am excited to see how many more lives will be transformed in the process.

Crossing Boundaries:

From Obsession to Acceptance

Before diving into this chapter, I want to extend my heartfelt gratitude to the individual whose journey you are about to read. This retired government officer has graciously allowed me to share his story—one of struggle, addiction, and eventual redemption. His courage in permitting me to write about his experience is deeply appreciated, especially as he chooses to remain anonymous. His willingness to open up, despite the personal nature of his story, is a testament to his strength and his desire to help others who might find themselves in similar situations.

While his identity will remain private, the lessons from his journey are shared with the hope of inspiring others to seek help, to heal, and to understand that no matter how dark things may seem, there is always a way forward.

*****

At 62, a recently retired government officer, he found himself facing a world far removed from the structured routines he had known for decades. It was the time of COVID-19, and chaos gripped the globe, forcing everyone indoors and into isolation. His life, once filled with the constant hum of meetings, reports, and delegating tasks to subordinates, had suddenly fallen silent. All those years, he had rarely touched his personal computer or laptop—he had always relied on others to get the work done, to manage the technology he never quite embraced. Now, in the solitude of retirement, with no office to command and no reports to review, he found himself alone with more time than he knew what to do with—and with that time, came the beginning of a dangerous habit he never saw coming.

A retired person's mindset is often like an open book, with blank pages ready to be filled again. Freed from the demands of routine work, they stand at a crossroads—where life, once rigid and predictable, now seems full of endless possibilities. For some, retirement becomes an exciting opportunity to rewire their habits, explore long-held interests, and rediscover passions they'd set aside. It's a time to re-integrate their schedule, embrace a newfound freedom, and perhaps finally tick off the things they'd always wanted to do but never had the time for. Life can feel like a blank canvas, waiting to be painted with experiences that bring joy and fulfillment.

But not everyone sees it that way. For many, retirement feels like stepping into an unfamiliar void. The structure and purpose they once found in their daily routine vanish overnight. There's a certain unease in waking up without a clear agenda, and for some, it becomes easy to retreat into a shell, believing that life, as they knew it, has ended. The mind resists this change, and a sense of emptiness, a vacuum, begins to form. It's not always easy to shift from years of structure and responsibility to an open, unplanned existence.

Yet, our man's story was different. His experience didn't follow the usual path. While the world was struggling with a pandemic, his retirement brought him to a crossroads he never anticipated—one that led him down a path not of exploration or fulfillment, but of an unexpected addiction that almost consumed him.

During the lockdown, confined to his home with little to occupy his mind, our man was nudged by a few of his friends into a world he had never explored before. These friends, also in their retired years, introduced him to the vast, unfiltered expanse of the internet—an unfamiliar territory he had barely touched in his professional life. They showed him how to access indecent videos, how to engage in questionable texting, and even encouraged him to indulge in age-inappropriate fantasies. It all seemed harmless at first, a bit of curiosity to pass the time, spurred on by their assurances that *everyone does it* and that *no one would ever find out*.

Amazed by what he found, he began to explore deeper. The more he watched, the more he indulged, not realizing how quickly he was falling into the trap of addiction. What started as innocent curiosity morphed into something darker, but in his mind, it all felt justified. His friends were doing it—what harm could there be in following their lead? His once-disciplined life was now being replaced by hours spent in front of a screen, caught up in a secret world of fantasies that seemed thrilling yet strangely isolating. Without realizing it, he crossed the line between occasional indulgence and full-blown addiction, unaware that his actions were wrong, anti-social, and destructive–because in his eyes, *if everyone else does it, why not me*?

His family was the heart of a simple, higher middle-class household, where values and traditions held strong. His wife, a gentle and devoted woman, had spent her life by his side, not just as a partner but almost as a devotee. She had always revered him, admiring his dedication and hard work throughout his government service. To her, he was the rock–the man who had provided stability, respect, and comfort for their family. Worldly matters and complexities never touched her; she trusted him implicitly, never questioning his decisions or actions.

*****

While the world was struggling with a pandemic, his retirement brought him to a crossroads he never anticipated—one that led him down a path not of exploration or fulfillment, but of an unexpected addiction that almost consumed him.

*****

Their daughter, now a poised and ambitious 25-year-old, was eagerly awaiting the results of her MBA exams. She was the pride of their family, a reflection of their values and hard work.

Aspiring to carve out her own path, she had always looked up to her father with admiration, seeing him as a figure of strength, someone whose achievements she hoped to emulate. She, too, was busy with her studies and future plans, yet always made time for the family she cherished.

In their home, no matter how busy life became, one ritual remained sacred—the dinner table. Every evening, without fail, they would gather there, sharing stories, laughter, and moments of quiet companionship. It was where they reconnected after the day's hustle, a place that grounded them, binding them together as more than just a family—this was their sanctuary. The warmth of those meals was not in the food alone, but in the comfort of each other's presence, the unspoken love that wrapped around their small world.

But beneath the calm, a storm was quietly brewing. The man, once admired for his discipline and commitment, was slowly drifting away, his attention diverted by the secret addiction he had developed. The family remained unaware, trusting in the strength of their bonds, never suspecting that the man they looked up to was struggling in silence, slipping into a life that threatened to shatter the very foundation of their togetherness.

But slowly, things began to spiral out of control, and his behaviour became impossible to ignore. The man who once took pride in his discipline and family values was now a shadow of himself. His laptop, once an afterthought, became his constant companion. He clutched it tightly to his chest, guarding it as if it held his very soul—right from the early hours of dawn until late into the night.

The once devoted family man, who never missed a meal at the dinner table, began withdrawing from the very heart of his home. Instead of sharing stories and laughter with his wife and daughter, he started asking for his meals to be served in his room, preferring isolation over the family warmth he once cherished.

*****

But beneath the calm, a storm was quietly brewing. The man, once admired for his discipline and commitment, was slowly drifting away, his attention diverted by the secret addiction he had developed.

*****

His daughter, perceptive and concerned, couldn't shake the growing unease. This wasn't the father she had known all her life—the man who valued family traditions and togetherness. His behaviour had shifted, and she could feel the tension hanging in the air. With each passing day, she watched him closely, the nagging feeling in her chest growing stronger. Something wasn't right.

And then, one day, the truth hit her like a crushing wave. After days of quiet observation, she finally discovered what her father had been indulging in. The sight was shocking—her father, a man she admired and respected, had been consumed by something she never expected. Her heart sank as the harsh reality set in. It was embarrassing, painful even, to confront the fact that the man she had idolized had fallen into such behaviour. But there it was, staring back at her—a hard truth she had no choice but to face.

In that moment, the world she knew came crashing down. How could this happen? How had he slipped so far without them noticing? The embarrassment mixed with anger, confusion, and sorrow. She knew that from this point forward, nothing would be the same. But she also knew that something had to be done, no matter how difficult the road ahead would be.

The day his daughter confronted him, her voice steady but laced with pain, was the moment everything shifted. She told him, calmly but firmly, that he needed help. At first, he couldn't believe what she was saying. To him, it seemed like a harmless indulgence—something everyone did. After all, his friends had normalized it, assuring him it was nothing to worry about. He felt blindsided by her accusation, utterly unaware of the damage he had caused to himself and the family he once held so dear.

But his daughter saw through the justifications. She wasn't angry anymore—just heartbroken, and determined to save him from sinking deeper. With a mixture of love and firmness, she told him he needed professional help. She didn't demand or force, but her words left no room for doubt. She recommended him to me, and though reluctant, he eventually agreed. This was the turning point—the moment where the veil of denial began to lift, however slowly.

From that day forward, their relationship changed. The father, once a figure of strength in the family, couldn't bring himself to look his daughter in the eyes for the next two years. The shame he carried weighed heavily on him, and every glance in her direction felt like a reminder of the depths he had fallen to. Communication between them became strained, awkward—no longer the easy conversations they once had. They spoke through indirect means, relying on chats or passing comments through the mother. Every message they exchanged seemed veiled, loaded with unspoken feelings, regrets, and hurt.

The journey toward healing had begun, but it was far from easy. Both father and daughter struggled to reconcile the love they still held for each other with the painful reality they now faced. Each step forward was difficult, as they navigated this new, fragile relationship, trying to find a way back to the trust they once shared. It was a journey fraught with silence, tension, and emotional wounds—but one that ultimately would lead them toward a deeper understanding, and perhaps, redemption.

When I first met him, what struck me the most was the complete absence of guilt. There was no sign of remorse, no acknowledgment that what he was doing was wrong. To him, it was all quite simple—he hadn't hurt anyone, he wasn't disturbing anyone, so why the fuss? He carried an air of justification, as though the behaviour that had driven a wedge into his family was nothing more than a private indulgence, a harmless escape.

*****

The father, once a figure of strength in the family, couldn't bring himself to look his daughter in the eyes for the next two years. The shame he carried weighed heavily on him, and every glance in her direction felt like a reminder of the depths he had fallen to.

*****

In those first two sessions, he sat in silence. He listened as I spoke, but didn't say a word. It wasn't avoidance–it was more like he genuinely didn't see the need to engage. He didn't feel guilty because, in his mind, there was nothing to be guilty about. After all, he hadn't directly harmed anyone, and his actions were confined to the privacy of his own world. This rationalization made it hard for him to see why everyone around him was so concerned. It became clear to me that the idea of needing help hadn't originated with him–it had been his daughter's insistence that finally brought him to me.

I learned that even agreeing to come had been a struggle for him. He wasn't ready, not really. It wasn't shame that held him back, but a fundamental disbelief that what he was doing was wrong. His daughter had pleaded with him, and out of love for her–perhaps mixed with a sense of duty more than understanding–he had agreed to sit down with me. But in those early sessions, there was no connection, no acknowledgment of the issue at hand. His mind remained closed off, still rooted in the belief that as long as no one was physically hurt, there wasn't a problem to solve.

He had given me a nickname –"*jailor*". In his mind, I was someone who interrogated him, someone who cornered him with questions, forcing him to confront uncomfortable truths. To him, I wasn't a guide, but an enforcer—a person whose job was to make him feel wrong for something he didn't believe was a problem. He even spoke about me to his friends, sharing his experiences in a half-joking manner, as though my sessions were just another obstacle he had to endure.

His friends, unsurprisingly, took his side. They didn't see the harm either. They encouraged him not to take me seriously, reinforcing the idea that this was all unnecessary. "You're only doing this because of your daughter," they would say. "Just go for the namesake, but don't let her get in your head." They advised him to attend the sessions, but to tune out, to keep the walls up, and dismiss whatever I said as irrelevant. In their eyes, I was simply someone appointed to disrupt their shared indulgences—someone trying to cast guilt where, in their view, none was needed.

For a while, that's exactly what he did. He came to our sessions on his daughter's insistence, but with no intention of engaging. The nickname "jailor" wasn't just a label—it reflected how he felt trapped by the idea that he was being judged for something that, in his world, was perfectly normal.

His daughter confided in me about a growing concern—he had started developing severe headaches, which we knew were the result of hours spent glued to his laptop screen. He was consuming more and more content, with no sense of time or restraint. What began as a hidden indulgence was now manifesting in physical symptoms that were impossible to ignore. The once-energetic father, who had always prided himself on his discipline and self-control, was now showing signs of wear and tear—his health was starting to unravel.

My approach with him centered around NLP (Neuro-Linguistic Programming), a method designed to shift his mindset and break the destructive patterns he had fallen into. I knew that to truly help him, I had to get him to see his behaviour from a completely new perspective—one that showed him not just the damage he was causing himself, but the long-term consequences for his family.

NLP was key in helping him reframe his thoughts. Instead of viewing his actions as harmless indulgence, I guided him to understand how his habit was silently eroding the very foundation of his relationships. Through techniques like anchoring, I helped him reconnect with positive emotions and memories, replacing the need for this destructive escape with a renewed focus on the things that truly mattered in his life.

It was a gradual process, shifting his mindset from denial to awareness. Step by step, he began to realize how this addiction could have spiralled into a disaster—alienating his family, breaking the bonds of trust, and causing irreversible damage to his relationships. My goal wasn't just to help him stop the habit, but to transform his thinking so he could see the bigger picture. Without intervention, this could have cost him everything.

In the end, it wasn't just about breaking the habit—it was about bringing him back to a place where he could rebuild, regain control, and reconnect with his family in a way that was meaningful and lasting.

I remember he was never consistent with his sessions. Unlike most clients who committed to weekly meetings, he only came once every fifteen days, and even then, only late at night—after 9:30 p.m., when his wife had already gone to bed. She remained completely in the dark about everything: his activities, the treatment, the counselling. She had no idea what was really going on behind closed doors. In her eyes, he was still the man she had always trusted, the devoted husband whose routine had simply changed with retirement.

His daughter, however, wasn't fooled. She knew the severity of the situation and kept a vigilant eye on him. She would check in after each session, demanding screenshots as proof of his attendance and gauging his seriousness about the process. It was her way of ensuring he was actually engaging in the therapy, and not just attending for appearances. She had even warned her mother, instructing her not to give him the laptop for extended periods, as his screen time was spiralling out of control.

For his wife, it was like dealing with a child pleading for a toy—he would ask for the laptop repeatedly, his insistence increasing with each request. She didn't understand the full weight of the situation, and from her perspective, it seemed like a harmless habit. But as his addiction deepened, his behaviour mirrored that of a restless child, unable to resist temptation.

But then, when it seemed like his access had been restricted, he found another way. He got a new number for his mobile phone, and with it, a new means to explore the same destructive content. The laptop restrictions didn't matter anymore—his phone became his new escape, a secret window into the world he was still reluctant to give up. His daughter's efforts to rein him in were met with new challenges, as his addiction found a way to slip through the cracks once again.

The next two years of treatment were anything but easy. Progress was painfully slow at first, and after six months, the success rate hovered at a mere 5%. It felt like we were barely scratching the surface of the problem. His resistance was strong—he wasn't ready to fully face the consequences of his actions. But then, a shift began. Bit by bit, the layers of denial started to peel away.

The turning point came when we moved beyond the surface behaviours and delved into the heart of the issue—his sense of self-respect, or rather, the slow erosion of it. He had spent years convincing himself that his actions weren't harmful, but when I brought his attention to the fact that he was betraying his own values, it struck a nerve. I made him confront the guilt he had buried deep down, the realization that he wasn't just indulging in something harmless—he was cheating on his wife in a way that went beyond physical actions.

It was this realization that shook him to his core. The idea that he, a man who had been admired for his dedication and integrity, was now betraying the very person who had stood by him for decades was too much to bear. The realization hit hard: if he continued down this path, he would destroy everything he had built—his family life, the trust of his wife, the respect of his daughter. His addiction wasn't just a personal indulgence; it was a ticking time bomb that could blow apart the foundation of his home.

Once he grasped the gravity of the situation, the results began to improve. Slowly, but surely, he started to understand the impact his actions were having—not just on himself, but on those he loved. It was no longer about just breaking a habit; it was about saving his family and restoring the dignity he had nearly lost.

Today, he has finally broken free from the grip of that habit and now leads a peaceful, fulfilling retired life. The man who once lost himself in the shadows of addiction has returned to the things that once brought him joy. He has rediscovered his love for writing—crafting stories, poems, *shaayris*, and even *haikus*. The creativity that had long been stifled has blossomed once again, giving him a new sense of purpose.

Now, he's the center of attention at family gatherings, but for all the right reasons. No longer hiding behind a screen, he shares his writing with pride, and his words have become a source of delight for those around him. Family and friends gather eagerly to hear his latest creations, and I'm told that he has become the person everyone looks forward to seeing—flaunting his passion for writing with a confidence that was once buried under guilt and shame.

What was once a dark chapter in his life has been replaced by a lightness, a sense of fulfillment that comes from embracing his true self. He's no longer haunted by his past, but instead, celebrates the present, surrounded by the love and admiration of his family, who are proud of the man he's become.

This case is a powerful reminder of how quickly life can take unexpected turns—how even the most disciplined and respected among us can find ourselves lost in the grip of destructive habits. It shows that no one is immune to the temptations that creep in, especially when we are vulnerable, isolated, or struggling to adapt to new phases of life. But it also tells a deeper story—one of hope, of the human capacity for change, and the transformative power of seeking help.

At the heart of this journey was the evolving relationship between a father and his daughter—a relationship that grew in maturity and depth, even as they navigated the most difficult of circumstances. His daughter, who had once seen her father as a figure of strength and guidance, now found herself in the role of protector, guiding him toward the help he didn't know he needed. Through patience, love, and determination, she became the catalyst for his healing, showing that even when the roles reverse, family bonds can endure and become stronger.

His wife, on the other hand, remained innocent and unaware for much of this journey—blind to the storm brewing beneath the surface. In her world, their life was a picture of simplicity, built on the quiet rituals and unspoken trust they had shared for decades. There were secrets, yes—those little cracks that families sometimes cover up to keep the peace—but this secret, had it remained hidden, could have destroyed everything. Her ignorance wasn't a failure; it was a testament to the faith she had in her husband, faith that thankfully wasn't misplaced in the end.

If this story teaches us anything, it's that no matter how deep the fall, there is always a way back. Recovery is possible, even when it feels like all hope is lost. The maturity shown by his daughter, the innocence of his wife, and the ultimate redemption of a man lost in his own shadows remind us that families can heal. All it takes is the courage to reach out, to ask for help, and to trust the process of healing. The road may be difficult, but it leads to something far greater—a life reclaimed, relationships restored, and a future filled with possibility.

From Trauma to Triumph:

Priyanka's Story of Strength

I first met Priyanka at the same NGO event where I had met Ritu. But unlike Ritu, Priyanka's presence immediately conveyed a much deeper, more palpable sense of pain. Priyanka's face told a story before any words were spoken—a story of rejection, trauma, and a life spent battling to be understood. The weight of emotions hung heavy in the air, and it was clear that Priyanka's journey had been far more turbulent.

Priyanka was born male in a small town in West Bengal, but from an early age, reality clashed painfully with the identity society imposed. Childhood was not just difficult for Priyanka—it was agonizing. Every day was a struggle to survive in a body and a world that didn't see the real Priyanka. The trauma carried had been festering for years, and by the time we met, it was as if the scars of the past were etched into every expression and every hesitant word.

When Priyanka was just ten-year old, he was sexually assaulted and raped by his neighbour. For five years he raped him repeatedly and if that wasn't enough, two of his friends also raped him. Fear gripped Priyanka so tightly that telling anyone felt impossible. The neighbour's threats were like chains, silencing Priyanka with the constant reminder—"Say nothing, or it will only get worse." Trapped in a cycle of fear and pain, Priyanka endured the abuse in silence, unable to find a way out.

The trauma ran deep, leaving Priyanka isolated, depressed, and battling an overwhelming darkness throughout childhood. Each day felt heavier than the last, the weight of the abuse suffocating any hope of normalcy. Years passed before Priyanka could finally gather the courage to speak up, hoping that sharing the truth with Priyanka's parents would bring relief, understanding, or even protection.

But when Priyanka finally broke the silence, the response was crushing. Instead of the support so desperately needed, Priyanka's parents dismissed the plea, unable to comprehend or accept the reality. "How could you be raped? You're a male," they said, brushing off the pain as though it were an impossibility. That rejection cut deeper than the abuse itself, leaving Priyanka devastated, feeling abandoned and invalidated by the very people who were supposed to protect and nurture.

The torment didn't end at home. In school, Priyanka faced relentless bullying and harassment, ridiculed by classmates for Priyanka's feminine mannerisms. Every day was a fresh assault on Priyanka's sense of self, as the other students made Priyanka the target of cruel jokes and constant taunts. The school, which should have been a place of learning and growth, became a battleground of humiliation and pain.

*****

The trauma ran deep, leaving Priyanka isolated, depressed, and battling an overwhelming darkness throughout childhood. Each day felt heavier than the last, the weight of the abuse suffocating any hope of normalcy.

*****

Priyanka dreaded going to school, waking up each morning with a knot of anxiety in Priyanka's chest, knowing that more ridicule awaited. But there was no choice. Coming from a family with a strong educational foundation, Priyanka had to continue. The weight of expectation kept Priyanka bound to the classroom, even though it felt like a prison.

College brought no reprieve. Instead of a fresh start, the pattern repeated. Priyanka became the center of attention, but for all the wrong reasons. Priyanka was once again at the heart of every joke, every bit of harassment, as students fixated on Priyanka's differences, turning them into fuel for their fun. The walls of higher education felt no different from those of school—a place where Priyanka was singled out, laughed at, and made to feel as though there was no escape from the torment.

Priyanka found solace only within the walls of home. It was the one place that offered a semblance of safety, a sanctuary from the cruelty of the outside world. Away from the relentless bullying, Priyanka could finally breathe, knowing that inside this space, there would be no mocking, no harassment. At home, there were no prying eyes, no pointed fingers—just a fragile peace that offered a brief escape from society's harsh judgments.

But the world outside was ruthless, far beyond what words could capture. Priyanka wasn't just laughed at—Priyanka was targeted. There were times when people threw cigarette butts, stones, and anything they could find at Priyanka, as though Priyanka's very existence was something they couldn't tolerate. Each assault was a fresh wound, deepening the sense of isolation and helplessness.

Finally, Priyanka took a significant step in the journey of self-acceptance by undergoing Hormone Replacement Therapy (HRT). This marked a turning point for Priyanka and the family. It was during this time that they began to truly understand—despite being born male, Priyanka had always possessed the mannerisms, behaviours, and internal sense of identity that aligned with being female. The reality of Priyanka's struggle became clearer, and the family's perception shifted from confusion to compassion.

*****

Priyanka found solace only within the walls of home. It was the one place that offered a semblance of safety, a sanctuary from the cruelty of the outside world. Away from the relentless bullying, Priyanka could finally breathe, knowing that inside this space, there would be no mocking, no harassment.

*****

Priyanka's father, in particular, stood by with unwavering support. He not only accepted Priyanka's identity but became a pillar of strength in rebuilding Priyanka's life. He extended his love in practical ways—helping to secure Priyanka's financial stability and guiding the development of a career path. In a show of care and encouragement, he even arranged for Priyanka to travel to Dubai, offering a much-needed break from the emotional and physical challenges that had defined so much of Priyanka's life.

For the first time, Priyanka was surrounded by a sense of understanding and belonging, with a family that no longer saw differences as barriers but as part of the unique person they loved and supported.

Priyanka felt as though the world had made up its mind about who Priyanka was, and that reflection was far from kind. But over time, through consistent therapy and the use of my regular techniques, we began to chip away at those layers of self-loathing.

Gradually, Priyanka became more comfortable with me, opening up and allowing the healing process to begin. One thing that Priyanka often mentioned—and appreciated deeply—was that I accepted Priyanka completely, just as Priyanka was. I never saw gender, caste, or class as barriers to human connection, and Priyanka felt this. There was no bias, no judgment. This unconditional acceptance created a strong sense of calmness and trust that allowed Priyanka to feel safe in my presence.

Through our sessions, I picked up on subtle non-verbal cues—body language, unspoken emotions—that guided me in how best to approach Priyanka's treatment. These cues became vital in our work together, helping me understand where Priyanka needed support most. It wasn't just about what was said; it was about what wasn't. The silent language of emotion often spoke louder than words, and it helped me guide Priyanka through the journey toward self-acceptance and healing.

Today, Priyanka stands as a testament to resilience and transformation. Priyanka has blossomed into a successful social worker and entrepreneur, creating a range of products like jute bags and hand-fans. What once seemed like an impossible journey has turned into a flourishing business, with Priyanka regularly participating in exhibitions and achieving considerable success.

*****

I never saw gender, caste, or class as barriers to human connection, and Priyanka felt this. There was no bias, no judgment. This unconditional acceptance created a strong sense of calmness and trust that allowed Priyanka to feel safe in my presence.

*****

One of Priyanka's proudest moments was walking the ramp at a fashion show in Pune, an experience I encouraged Priyanka to embrace. It wasn't just a walk–it was a powerful statement of self-acceptance and confidence, a celebration of all that Priyanka had overcome.

Today, Priyanka is not just self-sufficient, but also deeply grounded in the reality of who Priyanka is. Having embraced and accepted the path life has taken, Priyanka stands tall in a space of independence and strength. I continue to ask Priyanka to report to me periodically, not just for updates on professional success, but to share and reflect on life's journey–what's working, what challenges remain, and to ensure the emotional balance that is so crucial.

There are also exercises I've given Priyanka to maintain a healthy mindset, routines designed to keep Priyanka focused and in the right emotional zone. Priyanka diligently follows them, knowing that the journey toward self-care and mental well-being is ongoing. It's a joy to witness the person Priyanka has become, thriving in both business and life, while staying true to the work we've done together.

Today, Priyanka speaks with a heart full of gratitude and strength. Reflecting on the journey, Priyanka says, "Now, I can talk to Neeta ma'am, share my problems, because she is always there—behind me, beside me. She has been a constant source of inspiration and motivation." Priyanka further acknowledged "She taught me to trust in my own strength, helped me set goals, never judged me and guided me in working through my trauma. She showed me how to release the past and create something beautiful out of my life."

The bond between us has become a lifeline, one that Priyanka treasures deeply. "There have been times when I've called her unexpectedly, and each time, I've simply said, 'Priyanka, tell me... I'm here, just tell me. I will listen.' Those words—'I will listen'—they empower her. They make her feel that no matter what, I'm there for her.

Priyanka describes me as "a powerful counsellor," but it's so much more than that. It's the compassion, the patience, and the unshakable belief that has transformed Priyanka's life.

As Priyanka now stands, strong and self-reliant, it's clear that the journey has been one of hope, acceptance, and profound growth. Through all the challenges, there is a light that shines brighter than ever—a light that emerged from the shadows, one that will never be dimmed again. Priyanka's story is not just a testament to resilience but a beacon of hope for anyone struggling to find their own path. Because with the right support, even the darkest shadows can give way to light.

Embracing the Light:

Sona's Triumph Over Trauma

From a Worrier to a Warrior–this is the journey of Sona Banerjee, a woman who has battled against the formidable challenges of depression, anxiety, and bipolar disorder. Her life has been marked by the relentless ups and downs of these conditions, where each day has brought new struggles and unexpected victories. Sona's journey hasn't been easy, but it has been transformative. With courage, resilience, and a fierce determination to reclaim her life, she has transitioned from a place of constant worry to becoming a warrior–someone who faces her battles head-on with strength and hope.

This is the brave story of Sona Banerjee, a woman I first met in 2017 under difficult circumstances. She was brought into my husband, Dr. Srikant's clinic in a severely manic state, overwhelmed by depression and deep emotional turmoil. Her family—her mother-in-law, father-in-law, and husband—had come together, deeply concerned and desperate for help. The reason for their visit was critical: Sona had refused her anti-psychiatric injections, rejecting the medications she needed to stabilize her condition.

The weight of her struggle was evident, as was the worry in her family's eyes. This was more than just a visit to a clinic; it was a plea for support, a call to help Sona find a way out of the darkness that had consumed her life.

Dr. Srikant had long been the trusted family doctor for Sona's in-laws, which is why they had turned to him in this time of crisis. Recognizing the depth of Sona's needs, however, he referred her to me, knowing that she would benefit from focused therapeutic support. And that is how my journey with Sona began—a journey toward understanding, healing, and, ultimately, resilience.

Depression and anxiety—these are words that carry a quiet, hidden weight. Invisible to the naked eye, they reach deep into the core of a person, quietly impacting the most private corners of their being. Beneath the surface, these conditions create a constant, relentless struggle that is as exhausting as it is isolating. Left unaddressed, they can spiral into even darker places, leading to consequences that ripple through every aspect of life. It's a silent battle, but one that requires immense care and the right support to overcome.

I learned that Sona's depression and anxiety had taken root after a deeply personal setback and loss—a traumatic event that had shaken her world and left her struggling to find her way out. The incident weighed heavily on her, casting a shadow over her daily life and straining her relationships with those closest to her. While her own family, including her sisters and parents, rallied around her with unwavering support, the tension with her in-laws only grew. The disconnect within her immediate family, particularly with her in-laws, added to her emotional burden, intensifying the isolation she felt in the very place that should have offered solace.

*****

Depression and anxiety—these are words that carry a quiet, hidden weight. Invisible to the naked eye, they reach deep into the core of a person, quietly impacting the most private corners of their being.

*****

The first thing I did when Sona was brought to me was to gently hold her, offering her a sense of comfort and a momentary peace in the midst of her turmoil. She needed that human connection, a simple act of reassurance to remind her that she was safe. As I held her, my husband was able to administer the much-needed injection, which had been a challenge before. Within ten minutes, Sona began to settle, the immediate storm within her quieting, if only for a moment. Her family took her home shortly afterward, but I knew the calm we achieved that night was only temporary. It was just the beginning of a long journey ahead.

The next day was a Sunday, and by morning, we received word that Sona's behaviour had returned to the same distressed state as before. Her husband, feeling desperate, reached out to me directly, providing more details about her situation. Her psychiatrist was unavailable, and Sona remained resistant to any form of therapy or counselling, refusing the very support that could help her. I could sense the profound helplessness in his voice, a family grasping for a solution but unsure where to turn. The situation felt urgent, and I knew they were relying on me to guide them through this delicate and challenging moment.

My engagement with Sona soon became a regular part of her routine, as she grew more comfortable with me and discovered I was a therapist. This sense of familiarity allowed her to open up, and I could see the signs of her mood swings and heightened anxiety first-hand. Her bipolar symptoms, psychosis, and the complexities of postpartum and psychosomatic behaviour became clear as we spent more time together.

*****

The first thing I did when Sona was brought to me was to gently hold her, offering her a sense of comfort and a momentary peace in the midst of her turmoil. She needed that human connection, a simple act of reassurance to remind her that she was safe.

*****

One significant strain was her relationship with her mother-in-law, a dynamic that was deeply troubling for Sona. She confided in me about the tension between them, but others around her had dismissed it, telling her that friction with a mother-in-law was "nothing extraordinary" and "just the way things are." This lack of validation only deepened her frustration and self-doubt. At times, she would even ask me to speak with her mother-in-law, hoping that it might bring some sense of understanding and relief to a situation that felt impossible to navigate alone.

While Sona was already under medication prescribed by her psychiatrist, what she truly lacked was a therapist and counsellor—someone who could offer emotional guidance and a path toward inner peace. I took on the role of her therapist, focusing on creating a sense of calm and stability in her life. To support her healing, I introduced therapeutic practices like meditation, breathing exercises, journaling, and mandala painting, each designed to help her reconnect with herself. I gave her plenty of "homework" to reinforce these practices, encouraging her to establish routines that could ground her through the ups and downs.

Knowing how fragile her state was, I made myself exceptionally available to Sona, offering 24/7 support, even through chats while I was abroad. She needed that reassurance, someone who would listen without judgment, someone she could count on unconditionally. There were moments of deep trauma when a message or call wasn't enough, and I would visit her at home, just to be there in person and offer the support she so desperately needed. This was more than just therapy—it was a lifeline, and I was determined to be there for her, no matter the circumstance.

Sona's young daughter, Adhya, put on a brave face as she witnessed her mother's struggles. Initially, Adhya was frightened, overwhelmed by everything she was seeing and too young to fully understand. I knew I had to gently bring her into the journey—to help her make sense of her mother's condition and remove the lingering fear. My goal was to encourage Adhya's support, love, and understanding for her mother, nurturing a bond of compassion rather than worry.

Watching Adhya rise to this challenge was deeply moving. She embraced her role with a maturity far beyond her years, offering her mother gentle support and patience, the kind only a daughter could give. Her ability to adapt and empathize, especially at such a young age, was nothing short of remarkable. Today, at just eleven, Adhya continues to show an innate maturity, a steadfast resilience that is both inspiring and heart-warming. She has not only been a source of strength for her mother but a reminder to all of us of the incredible resilience children can possess when given love and guidance.

*****

Initially, Adhya was frightened, overwhelmed by everything she was seeing and too young to fully understand. I knew I had to gently bring her into the journey—to help her make sense of her mother's condition and remove the lingering fear.

*****

During this period, Sona's psychiatrist moved abroad, leaving her without a familiar support system for her treatment. This change unsettled her deeply; she felt as though the ground had shifted beneath her, unsure of how to cope with the abrupt loss of a trusted figure in her care. Recognizing her distress, I knew I needed to step in and provide stability during this challenging transition. I recommended another psychiatrist, someone who, coincidentally, had also been suggested by her previous doctor. This continuity offered Sona a sense of reassurance, helping her feel supported as she continued her journey toward healing.

I observed early on that Sona was deeply committed to her therapy, attending every session punctually and with genuine concern for her progress. She approached each step of the process with sincerity, determined to reclaim control over her life. Unfortunately, her in-laws did not share her faith in therapy. They frequently spoke against it, dismissing counselling as ineffective and attributing her struggles to unfavourable stars and destiny, convinced that her health issues were inevitable and unchangeable. Their words cast a shadow over her efforts, making an already challenging journey even more difficult.

In contrast, Sona's parents in Dehradun stood by her unwaveringly. They understood the importance of mental health care and encouraged her to stay committed to therapy with me, recognizing that it was a crucial part of her healing. Their support and understanding were a source of strength for Sona, counterbalancing the scepticism around her. With her parents' encouragement, Sona continued forward, unshaken by the doubts surrounding her, determined to create her own path to recovery.

Today, Sona and her family have moved to Noida, but she remains in touch, her spirit brighter than ever. She has overcome the shadows of her past, finding a sense of peace and positivity that once seemed unreachable. The demons that once haunted her have faded, replaced by a renewed outlook on life. Sona stands as a testament to the power of resilience, reminding us that with the right support and determination, healing is within reach.

*****

I observed early on that Sona was deeply committed to her therapy, attending every session punctually and with genuine concern for her progress. She approached each step of the process with sincerity, determined to reclaim control over her life.

*****

Sona's story is more than a journey of healing; it's a powerful reminder that no matter how deep the darkness may seem, there is always a way forward. With courage, patience, and the support of those who truly care, even the heaviest burdens can be lifted. Her path shines as a beacon of hope for anyone facing struggles of their own, reminding us that no matter how difficult the road, there is light, there is peace, and there is a future worth fighting for.

Productive Living with Practical Selfcare

1. Give yourself a break today. Instead of dwelling on the people who have let you down, refocus your energy on appreciating those who lift you up. Remember, **you can't change the impolite things some people say and do to you, but you can decide to choose. This is Power Of choice**.

2. Sometimes your mind needs more time to accept what your heart already knows. Pause, Breathe. **Give yourself the space to listen to your own voice.** Do not listen to the noise of the world, it's just chaos don't get lost in the crowd.

3. Be kind, but learn to say no. You can't always be agreeable. **Sometimes you have to set boundaries**. Sometimes saying no is vital self-care.

4. When life feels like an emotional roller coaster, just do **simple rituals**. Make the food. Do your bed. Water the plants. Rinse off your own bowl and spoon. Simplicity attracts calmness and wisdom.

5. Whatever you do, don't get stuck on the one little thing that wrecks your mood today. Breathe and be grateful for what's in front of you. Some of it is a blessing, and nothing lasts forever. **Life is just too short to waste on any negativity...or any negative self-talk too**.

6. No matter how long you've travelled in the wrong direction, you always have the choice to turn around. So, accept it, learn from it, and grow from it. It doesn't matter what you've done-what matters is what you do and where you go from here.

7. Dare to make edits and improvements. Dare to make your growth a priority. **The truth is, you won't always be a priority to others, and that's why you need to be a priority to yourself.** Learn to respect yourself, take care of yourself, and become your own support system. Your needs matter. Start meeting them...Don't wait on others to choose you. Choose yourself today.

8. You may have been broken down by adversity or rejection or stress, but YOU are not broken. You are not stuck!

So don't let your mind or anyone else try to convince you otherwise. Heal yourself, and grow beyond the default settings in life. Choose to take up a lot of positive space in your own life today. Choose to give yourself permission to meet your own needs honour your feelings and emotions. Choose to make self-care and personal growth top priorities and YES, I know that's much easier said than done, but you are not alone on this journey. Many of us are right there with you, working hard to do the right things for ourselves. Atleast you started.. You thought about your wellness, your selfcare.. Be happy !

Self-Care Tips-

1. Take a nap. Keep yourself hydrated.

2. Do something you've been wanting to do - and do it alone - instead of waiting for someone to do it with you.

3. Meditate, Journal your thoughts, just scribble...

4. Enjoy a cup of coffee, tea and your favourite book.

5. Take a shower or bubble bath with yummy smelling lotions.

6. Say no when you want to say no - so you have more time for a favourite "yes" activity.

7. Spend less time with people who drain you off - so you have more time for uplifting people.

8. Make room in your schedule for a favourite hobby - and literally schedule it - so you don't have (b)lame excuses not to do it.

9. Turn off your phone - unless you use it to watch funny videos.

10. Go for stroll, spend some Me time without gadgets.

11. Sing and dance to your favourite song!

12. Declutter your space.

13. Practice Affirmation - 'Affirm' means to validate or confirm:

    - I trust myself.
    - I am safe and loved.
    - I am powerful and blessed.
    - I believe in myself.
    - My breath and life is a gift.
    - I create joy everyday.
    - I take action and accomplish my goals.
    - I have faith in my abilities.

- Every opportunity is a possibility
- I am thankful for everything and everyone in my life.

13. Get into Gratitude Practice - Best Mantra
14. Get up and follow your routine
15. Don't forget to wear your smile as it suits you.
16. Adding a pinch of laughter will make your body energized.
17. Express yourself Creatively
18. Writing, Colouring, Doodling and just doing Strokes.
19. Remember that you are important - So turn illness to wellness.

#youmatter

#illnesstowellness

Epilogue:

As I reach the closing of this book, I am filled with a deep sense of gratitude for every individual who trusted me with their story, their vulnerabilities, and their courage. Each journey captured within these pages is a testament to the human spirit—a reminder that while life can be fraught with pain, loss, and struggles, there is always a pathway to healing.

Through the stories mentioned in this book and countless others, we see that the struggles we face do not define us. They may shape us, leaving marks we carry forward, but they do not have to limit us. Each of these individuals faced darkness, moments where hope felt distant, and fear took hold. Yet, they chose to confront their demons, seek help, and reach for a life beyond what they once thought possible. In the end, they found not only healing but also a renewed sense of purpose and resilience that became the foundation of their strength.

If there's one message I hope to leave you with, it's this: **you are not alone, and there is always hope**. Whether you are dealing with the complexities of mental health, navigating personal challenges, or facing circumstances that feel insurmountable, there is light to be found. Sometimes, it comes from within, sometimes from the support of loved ones, and sometimes, it emerges from the quiet courage to ask for help. Healing is a journey—a continuous process of growth, self-discovery, and forgiveness. It may not always be easy, but it is always possible.

This book is dedicated to those who are still struggling, to those who feel unseen, and to those who carry their battles in silence. My hope is that these stories have shown you that healing is not only possible but that it is your birth right. Let this be an invitation to reach out, to embrace your journey, and to know that there is always a way forward, **Beyond The Shadows**, toward a life filled with light, acceptance, and peace.

Thank you for joining me on this journey. May it inspire you to seek your own healing, to embrace your unique path, and to believe, as I do, that we each possess the strength to overcome.

Disclaimer:

The stories, experiences, and therapeutic approaches discussed in this book reflect the personal journeys of individuals who sought counselling with Dr. Neeta Mhatre. While these methods and insights proved effective for some, it is important to understand that everyone has unique coping mechanisms and experiences. There is no guarantee that the techniques or strategies mentioned will work for every reader. The content of this book is not intended as a substitute for professional medical, psychological, or therapeutic advice. Readers are encouraged to seek professional help tailored to their specific needs.

All stories are shared with the explicit consent and authorization of the individuals involved.